AUBREY BEARDSLEY:

Selected Drawings

AUBREY BEARDSLEY:

Selected Drawings

Grove Press, Inc.
New York

INTRODUCTION

Aubrey Beardsley did something to England, and to the English, from which they have never recovered. Unknown in 1892, and dead by the end of 1898, at age twenty-five, he had only a very little time in which to do it. All the omens were against his survival as an artist of any importance: he never went to art school, he never painted a big picture, he never had an exhibition. Most of his drawings were either for books which few people have ever seen or for magazines now known only to the historian. Yet of all the English reputations of the eighteen-nineties, his is certainly the strongest. More than 100,000 people crowded to see his work in London in the summer of 1966, and it is entirely possible that the Gallery of Modern Art will be similarly crowded when Beardsley gets his first full-scale showing in New York in February, 1967.

Beardsley died, as I have said, in 1898. By 1911, the shortcomings of Oscar Wilde's *Salomé* were obvious to everyone, but Beardsley's illustrations for that ridiculous playlet were as haunting as ever. The narrator in D. H. Lawrence's *The White Peacock* described the classic reaction to them when he said: "I sat and looked, and my soul leaped out upon the new thing. I was bewildered, wondering, grudging, fascinated..."

What Beardsley had done was to enlarge the notion of sexual response: the public was made aware of elements in its own nature which had hitherto been suppressed, consciously or otherwise. That was what Lawrence called "the new thing." It was promulgated in the eighteen-nineties, when the "manly wholesomeness" of Sir John Everett Millais had made art seem like a department of normality, and it has kept its thralldom intact into our own day. New Yorkers who are familiar, for instance, with the full-breasted giantesses who dominate the art of Richard Lindner should be in no doubt: those formidable ladies descend directly from Beardsley's Messalina.

By introducing the notions of fear and of tyranny and of insatiable appetite into the concept of female sexuality, Beardsley released feelings among his admirers for which no outlet had existed. He did this not as a pornographer but as a genuinely obsessed person who identified himself in his imagination with every one of the bizarre situations which got set down on the paper. More than any other English artist of his time, and more than most artists anywhere at any time, he knew how to answer the question "What can I do that no one else can do?" By answering it he won himself a place among the immortals. As Sir Kenneth Clark put it last year, "Beardsley is a small, hard, irreducible fact in the history of the human spirit."

Aubrey Vincent Beardsley was born in Brighton on August 21, 1872. He was the son of a marriage initiated by a chance encounter on Brighton Pier and pushed through to a rapid conclusion by Vincent Paul Beardsley and Ellen Agnus Pitt. The match had an air of solidity, in that Beardsley came of a long line of London jewelers and had substantial expectations, while Miss Pitt was the daughter and granddaughter of respected medical men. (I owe to Sir Kenneth Clark the information that "on account of her extreme slenderness, she was known as 'the bottomless Pitt.'") It turned out, however, that Vincent Beardsley had inherited tuberculosis and was unfitted for any kind of regular work. He very soon squandered his money. If it had not been for Mrs. Beardsley's talents as French-speaking governess and music teacher, Aubrey Beardsley and his sister, Mabel, would have been in a bad way from the start. As it was, he was barely seven when it was diagnosed that his father's tuberculosis had transferred itself to yet another generation.

Tuberculosis today is one of the toothless tigers of medicine, but in Beardsley's day it was an evil from which there was no lasting escape. One of its effects was a frantic acceleration of the creative energies, alternating with periods of physical prostration. Beardsley must have been aware at a very early age that he had not long to live. In school and out of it, he had a privileged status, and was excused from organized games, examinations, and many of the other chores of first youth. He could have foundered in invalidism; no one would have blamed him. But he displayed, on the contrary, an exceptional pertinacity. One witness said that "he never in a sense learned to read, but seemed to be perfectly conversant with the English language from the first moment of handling a book."

In his eleventh year, and thanks to lessons paid for by an aristocratic patroness, he was enough of a pianist to appear in public. He was as much at home in French as in English literature. Attracted in his boyhood by Kate Greenaway's vision of childhood as expressed in her illustrations in water color, he mimicked these with such skill that he was soon supplementing the family income by the sale of designs for menu cards.

Above all, Beardsley was theater-struck. While still at school, he could address an audience of 3,000 people and command their attention absolutely. He wrote plays and performed in them with the utmost relish (his sister later went on the stage), and the family's theatrical evenings in London and elsewhere were always a great success. Beardsley was young at a time when the great performers, whether in opera or in the spoken theater or in vaudeville, were genuinely "larger than life." Reputations could not be faked up on film or with doctored phonograph records; everything had to be done, and seen to be done, by direct contact with the audience. Beardsley learned a great deal from these people about the projection of personality, and about the importance of an absolute technical command and about the elimination of superfluous detail. English art in general had become timid, fussy, evasive, and overupholstered. Beardsley brought to it the kind of ruthlessness which an actress like Réjane brought to French tragedy or a singer like Katharina Klafsky brought to Wagner's Isolde.

Beardsley was secretive about his methods of his work, and would at once hide his materials if anyone came into the room. But there was nothing secretive about the work when it was released. He had the gift of going straight to the point. One of his classmates in school was C. B. Cochran, later to be the greatest English impresario of his day, and Cochran for the rest of his life remembered Beardsley as a boy built for success.

But the best that could be done for Beardsley when he left school at the age of sixteen was a stool in the office of the borough surveyor in Clerkenwell, North London. It was, if anything, providential that in the fall of 1889, he began to spit blood. "My heart is so weak," he wrote a week or two later, "that the least exertion brings on a bad hemorrhage. My Christmas has been on slops and over basins. Of course, I have to leave the office. I read all day..."; and a sketch on the facing page shows him propped up in a high-backed armchair, in front of a blazing fire, with some prize specimens of Victorian library furniture to keep him comfortable.

What was he dreaming about? Not, quite certainly, the "decadent" writers of his own day. Beardsley's tastes were of an altogether tougher, heavier, more enduring sort. Even at the height of his fame he was more likely to ask for Dr. Johnson's English dictionary, or for a two-volume life of Goethe, than for the epicene fancies which passed for decadence in England. Beardsley may have shaped the spirit of his age, but he was never its creature.

He had personal attractions which few people could resist. But, there again, those attractions were incidental to a powerful and systematically developed intelligence. After his death, his friends vied with one another in describing his phantomatic manner of gliding into the room, his stylized and emphatic manner of speech, and his way of brushing his long hair flat and forward so that it overhung his immensely high and narrow brow.

Robert Ross, who first met him in 1892, wrote that "he had a most delightful and engaging smile, both for friends and for strangers. He was full of Molière and *Manon Lescaut.* At the same time he seemed disappointed that none of us was musical; his knowledge of Balzac astonished an authority on the subject who was present. He spoke much of the National Gallery and the British Museum, both of which he knew with extraordinary thoroughness..."

Beardsley himself made light of it all. "I am now 18 years old," he wrote in 1890, "with a vile constitution, a sallow face and sunken eyes, long red hair, a shuffling gait and a stoop." This was at a low point in his affairs, however, and from the moment when he finally decided that drawing was the true outlet for his gifts life showered upon him the kind of good luck without which it is difficult for a young artist to get started. Burne-Jones, for instance, was the hero at that time of most young people of sensibility: "The greatest artist in Europe" was Beardsley's own estimate of him. Calling on Burne-Jones under the mistaken impression that casual visitors were welcome, he was turned away from the door, only to have Burne-Jones himself run down the street after him. Once inside the house, he was given tea, confirmed in his vocation and introduced to Oscar Wilde. "I seldom or never advise anyone to take up art as a profession," said Burne-Jones, "but in your case I can do nothing else."

When Dent, the publisher, was planning an illustrated edition of Malory's *Morte d'Arthur,* Beardsley got the job as a result of a chance meeting with Dent in a book-store. Hardly had he signed his contract with Dent than he met someone who was planning a new art magazine, *The Studio,* and when the first issue of that famous magazine came out in September, 1893, Beardsley, then just turned twenty-one, was the subject of a lengthy and eulogistic article. When he went to Paris in the summer of 1892, he had few claims upon anyone's attention; but Puvis de Chavannes, then president of the Salon and one of the best-known painters in the world, introduced him to his friends as "a young Englishman who is doing astonishing things."

As I have tried to indicate, Beardsley was both in his time and out of it. He was as likely to lift an idea from Dürer or Pollaiuolo as from the beginnings of *art nouveau,* and his mature work owes as much to Greek vase painting as to anything done in his own day. People who go to him for "period detail" are both right and wrong: right in that he had a highly developed parodistic sense and could not draw a tree or a piece of furniture or a woman's dress without making a critical comment on the styles of the time; wrong because Beardsley never cared anything at all for "authenticity" or for coherence of idiom. He was such a master of isolated detail that whatever he chose to emphasize became unforgettable; but Beardsley is a guide to Beardsley, not to *art nouveau* or to the esthetic movement or to English decadents.

His mother's mother had been a gifted silhouettist, but Beardsley himself began as a draftsman, in the style of Burne-Jones and William Morris: a maker, in other words, of penciled tapestries derived at many removes from Botticelli. The rhythms of these were languid and slack, and he followed his masters' tendency to put in everything, leaving no corner of paper unfilled. But in December, 1892, he wrote that in the future he would devote himself to "fantastic impressions treated in the finest outline with patches of 'black blot.'"

To a friend he wrote: "How little the importance of line is understood! It is this feeling for harmony in line that sets the old masters at such an advantage to the moderns, who seem to think that harmony in color is the only thing worth attaining."

Beardsley's posters prove, as a matter of fact, that he was a gifted and original colorist, and the equal, in this relatively new medium, of a Bonnard or a Toulouse-Lautrec. But the thing which made him world-famous in a year or two was his mastery of outline used in conjunction with the blackest blacks and the whitest whites that the printing press could provide. It was an art which, as Arthur Symons said, was meant to pull people up short. Beardsley's posters, Symons went on, were "art meant for the street, for people who walk fast"; and his published drawings aimed at the same instantaneous effect. They were theater, quintessentialized. Beardsley placed his figures as a great actor places the key phrase in a speech. There were echoes of other artists, from Mantegna to Whistler, and echoes of the new decorative styles that were going through Europe like Spanish influenza, but the name of Beardsley soon stood for something specifically his own, in which style and concept were one.

This was especially the case when, from April, 1894, onward, Beardsley's drawings appeared in number after number of *The Yellow Book*. Such is the reputation of this magazine that one might think it to have been a pornographic anthology in which text and illustrations vied with one another as to which could be the more indecent. In point of fact, the stories, essays, and poems in *The Yellow Book* were no more pornographic than the stories, essays, and poems in *Harper's* or *The Atlantic Monthly*. *The Yellow Book*'s reputation was owed entirely to Beardsley's drawings and to his role as art editor. Nothing like these incisive, disquieting, and unscrupulous little works had ever been seen in England before. Among them was one of Beardsley's masterpieces, "The Wagnerites," in which the audience for *Tristan und Isolde* is represented as made up almost entirely of predatory, bare-shouldered giantesses who have no need of male company.

This kind of thing tried the nerves of a large section of our English public and caused them to feel, quite rightly, that they were being got at. A reaction was bound to come, and it came when, in April, 1895, Oscar Wilde was arrested at the Cadogan Hotel and the whole of London was swept by wave after wave of righteous feeling. As a matter of fact, Wilde disliked *The Yellow Book* and had never written for it. He and Beardsley were friends in a general way, and there does exist a post card, dated April, 1893, which ends with the words "I'm off to Paris soon with Oscar Wilde," but the extent of their intimacy has never been proved and there was nothing to link them directly at the time of Wilde's arrest.

The newspapers reported, however, that when the police came to fetch him, Wilde had "grasped his suede gloves in one hand, seized his stick with the other and placed a copy of *The Yellow Book* in security under his left arm." This was once again a misapprehension, the reporter having actually said "a yellow book" (it was a paperbound copy of Pierre Louÿs's *Aphrodite*), but this was quite enough to set off a ferocious response. Mobs went round to *The Yellow Book* offices and broke all the windows. William Watson, a poet much in favor at the time, cabled the publisher of *The Yellow Book*: "Withdraw all Beardsley's designs or I withdraw all my books. Watson." And Beardsley was, in fact, summarily dismissed, and never appeared again in *The Yellow Book*.

For someone who had never had anything like security and was, indeed, never to have it, this was an unpleasant experience. It may well have persuaded Beardsley that both in life and in his art he would have to go underground. When, for instance, a new review was mooted in 1897, Beardsley promised full support "if it is quite agreed that Oscar Wilde contributes nothing to the magazine, anonymously, pseudonymously or otherwise." This was not pretty behavior, but it indicates the extent of Beardsley's anxiety.

After the disaster of *The Yellow Book* he never had a regular source of income from his work, and he fell into the hands of men like Leonard Smithers, who operated in the middle ground which separates reputable from disreputable publishing. Smithers encouraged him to release some of his deepest and most private feelings in illustrations for Juvenal and Aristophanes. On his deathbed Beardsley implored Smithers to "destroy all copies of *Lysistrata* and bad drawings. By all that is holy, all obscene drawings..." But there is no doubt that these drawings express something indispensable to Beardsley, and that they came about at a time when he felt himself an outcast from society in respect of that side of his nature.

This is a problem which has changed entirely since Beardsley's day. In the eighteen-nineties the exciting thing was to break down convention and to admit to the canons of art subject matter which the polite world had never dreamed of accepting. In our own time the difficult thing is, rather, to re-endow that subject matter with a certain poetic quality. The convention of our day is that anything can be said if it is said in a particular flat, documentary tone of voice. A deflationary idiom is believed to rob anything of offense. Beardsley, in this sense, has sat the program round. His work awed people in the eighteen-nineties, and it is awing them again today.

How far he himself was sexually active remains an open question. Brian Reade, in the catalogue of the London exhibition, conjectures that he may have been intimate with his own sister. There is also a suggestion, in the same catalogue, that he may have had a natural son. As to his homosexuality, there is no lack of innuendo.

People have claimed, also, that after Wilde's arrest Beardsley damaged his health still further by untimely attempts to prove that he was heterosexual. Certainly, toward the end of his life he was preoccupied with sex to a degree that probably indicated the falling-off, or extinction, of his own sexual powers. ("Even my teeth are a little phallic," he wrote in 1896.)

Perhaps, in any case, he despaired of total fulfillment. "I am still," he once wrote to Smithers, "the same old hard-working solitaire you know so well." The use of this rare noun may remind us that in his novel *Under the Hill* he wrote of one of its characters: "What were his amatory tastes, no one could tell. He generally passed for a virgin, and Cathos had nicknamed him 'The Solitaire.'"

Beardsley's was a disruptive and a subversive nature where sex was concerned, but he never put forward the view, so common among homosexual writers and painters of later date, that women are an unmixed curse who deserve to be punished simply for existing. On the contrary, he gave a rare intensity and authenticity to the idea of female sexual prowess. His favorite figure in this context was the masterful woman of mature years, the bare-breasted, full-bottomed tyrant who turns up over and over again and can be found, seen from behind and below, on Beardsley's own bookplate. (She is, of course, one of the resident demons of the homosexual imagination.) He goes on to imply that women take more pleasure in their own company, as sexual partners, than they do in men's, and that for that reason men would do well to leave them to it — and, by implication, to follow their example. Such was the hold of this idea upon his imagination that he imported it even into a poster which was meant to work for an understanding of the points of matrimony.

Beardsley's continuing fame is due in part to the eloquence with which he puts forward once-forbidden opinions. But his was a triumph of style as much as of content. The influence which he exerted all the way from New York to Moscow, not long after his death, was owed to the way in which he cut through the whole apparatus of outmoded pictorial vision and arrived at a simplified and frankly arbitrary presentation of the facts. If it bored him to put in the background, he left it out. If an important element in the design was masked by one of the figures in it, he just made that figure transparent. He didn't care about "proportion" or "perspective." He went all out for the main effect, and he knew that if the line had enough energy, observers would forgive everything else.

This was what attracted Picasso in his pink period, when the Barcelona magazine *Joventut* was boosting Beardsley. If Beardsley had not been featured in *The Studio* and elsewhere, German expressionist graphics would have been very different. The decorative arts, all over Europe, took something from Beardsley: in Paris, in Brussels and in Vienna you can see buildings to this day which would not be quite the same if someone had not pored over Beardsley.

His was an art of decisive effect, with "No compromise!" as its motto, and there was nothing weak or effeminate about the resolution with which he pursued it. This was what commended him even to artists like Paul Klee, who disliked the content of his drawings; and it is what would go on commending him even if the problems of sexuality, normal or abnormal, should one day seem as archaic as the struggles of Guelph and Ghibelline.

—John Russell

London, 1967

AUBREY BEARDSLEY:

Selected Drawings

1. DESIGN FOR TITLE PAGE OF SALOMÉ BY OSCAR
WILDE (JOHN LANE, 1894)

2. BORDER DESIGN FOR CONTENTS OF SALOMÉ

3. THE WOMAN IN THE MOON, 1893

From *Salomé*. A companion to "A Platonic Lament," in the same book. Note Wilde's portrait in the moon. There are other caricatures of Wilde in "Enter Herodias" and "The Eyes of Herod."

4. THE PEACOCK SKIRT, 1893

From *Salomé*. A drawing strongly influenced by the Japanese print by way of Whistler's Peacock Room, which Beardsley had visited and described at length in a letter to a friend.

5. A PLATONIC LAMENT, 1893

From *Salomé*. The "little green flower," which Salomé promises to let fall for the young Syrian, was a symbol often used by Wilde.

6. JOKANAAN AND SALOMÉ, 1893

Intended for *Salomé,* but suppressed from the first edition;
however it was included in later printings. The curving lines
serve in place of a realistic perspective.

7. THE BLACK CAPE, 1893

From *Salomé*. This drawing, a caricature of the fashion of the period, has no connection with the play except Salomé's fan, and was inserted to replace a suppressed drawing.

8. ENTER HERODIAS, 1893

First version. A caricature of Wilde in the foreground. In the original drawing the right-hand figure was nude, as shown here, and the artist afterward drew in the fig leaf for the published drawing.

On some proofs of the first version he wrote:

Because one figure was undressed,
This little drawing was suppressed,
It was unkind, but never mind,
Perhaps it was all for the best.

9. THE EYES OF HEROD, 1893

From *Salomé*. Herod to Salomé: ". . . thou knowest my white peacocks, my beautiful white peacocks, that walk in the garden between the myrtles and the tall cypress trees . . ."

It has been said that the peacock and the butterfly were symbols as well as forms of the grotesque for Beardsley. The butterfly originated with Whistler's signature device, said to have evolved from his initials JMW.

10. THE TOILETTE OF SALOMÉ I, 1893

Intended for *Salomé*, but suppressed. One of Beardsley's favorite themes. Note the Japanese furniture.

11. THE TOILETTE OF SALOMÉ II, 1893

This drawing was substituted for the previous one.

12. THE STOMACH DANCE, 1893

Neither the foreground of this drawing nor that of "Enter Herodias" was ever censored, though so many of Beardsley's drawings were. The absence of perspective, a characteristic borrowed from the Japanese print, remains present in subsequent periods of Beardsley's work.

13. THE DANCER'S REWARD, 1893

The shape of the "silver charger" supported by the executioner's arm rising from the cistern is also suggested in the drawing, "The Climax."

14. **SALOMÉ WITH JOHN THE BAPTIST'S HEAD**, sometimes "J'ai baisée ta bouche, Iokanaan."

Published with a selection of Beardsley's drawings in *The Studio*, No. 1, April, 1893, to illustrate an article by Joseph Pennell, "A New Illustrator"; it brought Beardsley the commission to illustrate *Salomé*. See following drawing.

15. THE CLIMAX, 1893

In a letter to Ross, around July, 1893, Beardsley says that one of the drawings he is making for *Salomé* is "*The Studio* picture redrawn and immensely improved." All inessentials removed, the drawing now exists solely through its own inner cohesion.

16. TAILPIECE (CUL-DE-LAMPE), 1893

From *Salomé*. In Ross's words ". . . a real masterpiece and a witty criticism of the play as well."

17. SALOME ON SETTLE, 1893

Intended for the book but suppressed. It is also called "Maitresse d'orchestre."

18. ALI BABA, 1897

For a projected edition of *Ali Baba and the Forty Thieves.*
Another example of Beardsley's skill in suggesting opulence,
as in some *Volpone* drawings, "The Wagnerites," or "The
Mysterious Rose Garden."

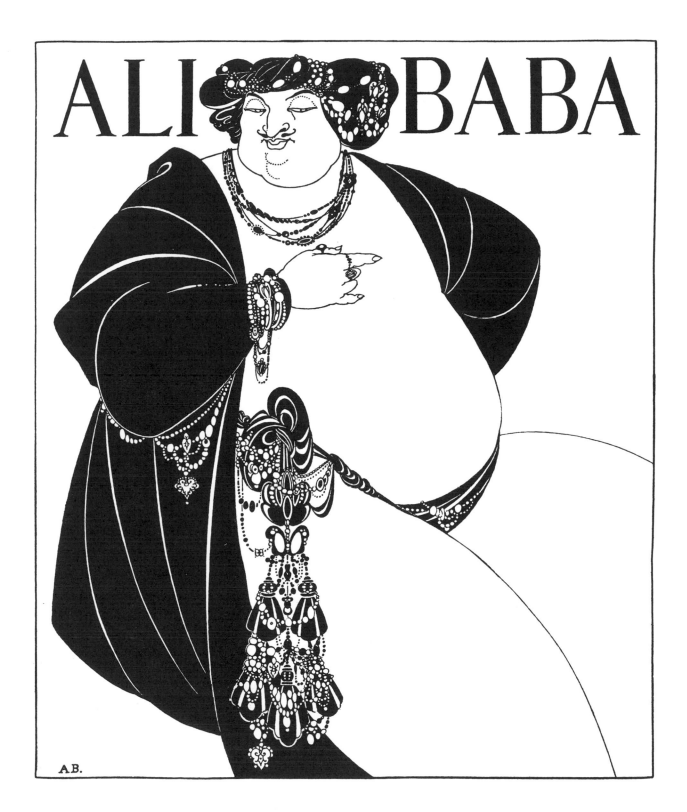

19. THE KISS OF JUDAS, 1893

From the *Pall Mall Magazine*, July, 1893. Very much in the spirit of the *Salomé* drawings, playing off the contrast between the beautiful and the grotesque, with its fanciful design and execution of the lettering against the triad motif, the details suggesting mystery.

THE KISS OF
JVDAS

20. FRONTISPIECE TO PLAYS BY JOHN DAVIDSON, 1893

This contains caricatures of Augustus Harris, Wilde, Genée, Mabel Beardsley, and Richard LeGallienne.

21. LADY GOLD'S ESCORT, 1894

From *The Yellow Book*, Vol. III. Satire, and typically discreet understatement in the suggestion of the Lyceum Theatre.

22. THE WAGNERITES, 1894

From *The Yellow Book*, Vol. III. As in the previous drawing, satirical content is allied to technical brilliance to suggest glowing light in a dark atmosphere.

23. LA DAME AU CAMELIAS, 1894

From *The Yellow Book,* Vol. III. Beardsley, who had a great fondness for this novel, later made another drawing of the same subject on the flyleaf of the copy given to him by Dumas *fils,* whom he had visited in Puys, near Dieppe, in 1895.

24. NIGHT PIECE, 1894

From *The Yellow Book,* Vol. I. The famous "broken black" technique.

25. LES PASSADES, 1894

From the winter number of *To-Day*, November 17, 1894.

26. COVER DESIGN FOR THE YELLOW BOOK, VOL. II, 1894

A bold design, printed in black on bright yellow cloth. The color was chosen to exploit the appeal of the popular detective novels which were bound in yellow.

27. COVER DESIGN FOR THE YELLOW BOOK, VOL. III, 1894

The incongruous addition of street lamps to the dressing table infuriated critics.

28. PORTRAIT OF HIMSELF, 1894

From *The Yellow Book*, Vol. III.

29. COMEDY-BALLET OF MARIONETTES I, 1894

From *The Yellow Book*, Vol. II. The artist's only painting in oil is a version of this drawing, now in the Tate Gallery, London, and now known as "A Caprice."

30. COMEDY-BALLET OF MARIONETTES II, 1894

From *The Yellow Book,* Vol. II

31. COMEDY-BALLET OF MARIONETTES III, 1894

From *The Yellow Book,* Vol. I. The central female figure was cut out and renamed "The Black Domino," and it was also named "Dancer with the Domino" when it was exhibited at the International Society's Exhibition of Fair Women, 1909.

32. GARÇONS DE CAFÉ, 1894

From *The Yellow Book,* Vol. II. One of Beardsley's most vigorous and realistic drawings, showing a bold treatment of perspective.

33. L'ÉDUCATION SENTIMENTALE, 1894

From *The Yellow Book*, Vol I. This drawing caused a great stir at the time. In a later version, only the left-hand figure remained, the drawing was retinted and renamed "Mrs. Marsuple," after the character in Beardsley's novel *Under the Hill* (which was at first called *Priapusa*) who can also be seen in "The Toilet of Helen."

34. MADAME RÉJANE, 1894

From *The Yellow Book,* Vol. II. One of many drawings of the great French actress whom Beardsley knew personally.

35. DESIGN FOR COVER OF THE DANCING FAUN, 1893

36. THE MYSTERIOUS ROSE GARDEN, 1894

From *The Yellow Book,* Vol. IV. Another "*éducation senti-
mentale,*" said to be Beardsley's idea of the Annunciation.

37. SIEGFRIED, 1893

Appeared in *The Studio* with the first article on Beardsley by
Joseph Pennell.

38. MERLIN, 1893

From *Le Morte d'Arthur* by Sir Thomas Malory (published by J. M. Dent) designed to compete with the editions of William Morris.

39. OF A NEOPHYTE, AND HOW THE BLACK ART WAS REVEALED UNTO HIM BY THE FIEND ASOMUEL, 1893

Illustration to a story of the same name in the *Pall Mall Magazine,* June, 1893. Shows the influence of the cult for things Japanese in the nineties.

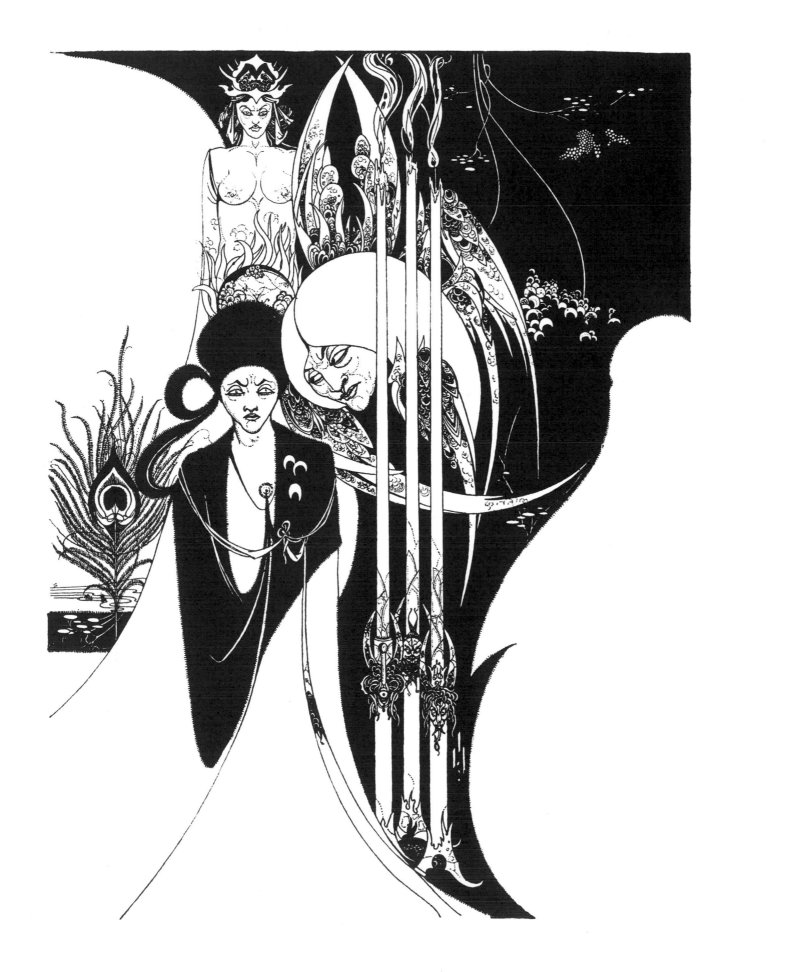

40. DREAMS

From Lucian's *True History* (Laurence and Bullen, 1894, privately printed). The drawings for the *True History* form a very heterogeneous series showing an evolution in Beardsley's style and met with a mixed response on publication.

41. A SNARE OF VINTAGE

From Lucian's *True History*, 1894. This illustration was inserted loose in the large format edition only, and replaced by the following drawing.

42. A SNARE OF VINTAGE

Another drawing of the same name. From Lucian's *True History*, 1894.

43. LUCIAN'S STRANGE CREATURES, 1894

Drawing for Lucian's *True History*. Never so used. A detail of
it was published in *The Early Work of A. B.*

44. BIRTH OF THE CALF OF THE LEG, 1894

Drawing for Lucian's *True History*. Not so used.

45. DESIGN FOR THE INVITATION FOR THE OPENING
MEETING OF THE PRINCES LADIES' GOLF CLUB,
MITCHAM, 1894

46. DESIGN FOR THE COVER OF POOR FOLK, 1893

47.   A POSTER, 1894

48.   A POSTER DESIGN, 1894

49. THE MURDERS IN THE RUE MORGUE

From *Tales of Edgar Allan Poe* (Stone and Kimball, Chicago, 1895).

50. THE BLACK CAT

From *Tales of Edgar Allan Poe* (Stone and Kimball, Chicago 1895).

51. THE FALL OF THE HOUSE OF USHER

From *Tales of Edgar Allan Poe* (Stone and Kimball, Chicago, 1895).

52. THE MASK OF THE RED DEATH

From *Tales of Edgar Allan Poe* (Stone and Kimball, Chicago, 1895).

53. ATALANTA I, 1895

One of two drawings on the same subject. The earlier drawing (without hound) was intended for *The Yellow Book,* Vol.
V.

54. ATALANTA II, 1897

Beardsley acknowledged to Smithers, his last publisher, that this made fun of Swinburne's famous tragedy "Atalanta in Calydon."

55. THE MIRROR OF LOVE, 1895

From *Aubrey Beardsley* by Arthur Symons (Unicorn Press, 1898). The drawing was probably intended as a frontispiece to a book by André Raffalovitch.

56. FRONTISPIECE, 1895

From *The Full and True Account of the Wonderful Mission of Earl Lavender*, by John Davidson, a satirical novel on London mores (Ward and Downey, 1895).

57. FRONTISPIECE, 1895

From *An Evil Motherhood* by Walt Ruding (Elkin Matthews, 1895). Replaced the following drawing.

58. BLACK COFFEE, 1895

Intended as a frontispiece for *An Evil Motherhood,* but rejected because of its suggestiveness. Was bound up in six review copies only.

59. LADY READING ON SOFA, 1896

Design for the wrappers of Leonard Smithers' fifth *Catalogue of Rare Books*. The striped sofa is a reminder of the famous décor of Beardsley's Pimlico flat, in orange and black.

60. COVER DESIGN FOR THE YELLOW BOOK PROSPECTUS FOR VOL. V, 1895

Not used in Vol. V, instead printed for Smithers' *Catalogue of Rare Books*.

61. COVER DESIGN, 1894

For *The Cambridge ABC,* an undergraduate magazine.

62. A SUGGESTED REFORM IN BALLET COSTUME

From *A London Garland*, Macmillan, 1895. Also called "At a Distance."

AUBREY BEARDSLEY.

63. THE REPENTANCE OF MRS.***, 1894

From *The Yellow Book,* Vol. IV. This is a new version, in a later manner, of an earlier drawing, "The Litany of Mary-Magdalen," which showed traces of the first influences on Beardsley, chiefly Mantegna and Burne-Jones. The theme is a favorite one of Beardsley's and the figure of Mrs.*** also resembles the dominant figure in an early drawing made to illustrate Zola's novel *La Faute de l' Abbé Mouret.*

64. THE DREAM, 1895-96

Belinda still her downy pillow pressed,
The guardian sylph prolonged the balmy rest:
'Twas he had summoned to her silent bed
The morning dream that hovered o'er her head.

from *Rape of the Lock* (Smithers, 1896).

Although Pope was at the time considered as the very anti-thesis of poetry, his heroic-comic poem, written to reconcile two families, was much enjoyed by Beardsley, who understood its wit and supplied what dreamlike grace it may have lacked.

65. THE BILLET-DOUX, 1895-96

'Twas then, Belinda, if report say true,
Thy eyes first opened on a billet-doux;

from *Rape of the Lock* (Smithers, 1896).

66. THE TOILET, 1895-96

And now, unveiled, the toilet stands displayed,
Each silver vase in mystic order laid.
from Rape of the Lock (Smithers, 1896).

As in the following drawing, note the treatment of the floor. The Claude-like parks, such as the one on the screen and in several drawings of this series, are often found in *The Savoy* drawings as well as in the descriptions of landscape in Beardsley's novel *Under the Hill*.

67. THE BARON'S PRAYER, 1895

On twelve vast French Romances, neatly gilt
There lay three garters, half a pair of gloves,
And all the trophies of his former loves;

from Rape of the Lock (Smithers, 1896).

68. THE BARGE, 1895-96

Launched on the bosom of the silver Thames.
Fair nymphs, and well-dressed youths around her shone,
But ev'ry eye was fixed on her alone.

from *Rape of the Lock* (Smithers, 1896).

69. THE RAPE OF THE LOCK, 1895-96

He takes the gift with reverence, and extends
The little engine on his fingers' ends;
This just behind Belinda's neck he spread,
As o'er the fragrant steams she bends her head.

from *Rape of the Lock* (Smithers, 1896).

A superb example of Beardsley's newly-acquired skill in suggesting the texture of any substance by line alone.

70. THE CAVE OF SPLEEN, 1895-96

Umbriel, a dusky, melancholy sprite,
As ever sullied the fair face of light,
Down to the central earth, his proper scene
Repaired to search the gloomy cave of Spleen.

from *Rape of the Lock* (Smithers, 1896).

As later drawings will show, this is a deliberate attempt, not yet fully successful, to express space only by means of a different treatment of each element in the drawing. This particular problem will find its triumphant solution in the design "The Abbé."

71. THE BATTLE OF THE BEAUX AND THE BELLES, 1895-96

To arms, to arms! the fierce virago cries,
And swift as lightning to the combat flies.
All side in parties, and begin th' attack
Fans clap, silks rustle, and tough whalebones crack;

from *Rape of the Lock* (Smithers, 1896).

Here, perfect balance between light and dark.

72. THE NEW STAR, 1895-96

A sudden star, it shot through liquid air,
And drew behind a radiant trail of hair.

from Rape of the Lock (Smithers, 1896).

73. COVER DESIGN, 1895

For *The Savoy*, No. I, 1895. Beardsley's reaction to his dismissal from *The Yellow Book* in 1895. The book in the foreground which Amor is sprinkling, was later removed.

THE SAVOY

AUBREY BEARDSLEY: 1896.

74. THE THREE MUSICIANS II, 1895

An illustration to his poem of the same name. Was omitted from *The Savoy,* No. I.

75. ON DIEPPE BEACH (THE BATHERS), 1895

A recollection of the favorite resort of the English Decadents, particularly of *The Savoy* group, and where Beardsley wrote most of his novel *Under the Hill*.

76. MOSKA, 1895

From *The Savoy*, No. I. As the drawing before, an illustration for Arthur Symons' article on Dieppe in this issue of *The Savoy*.

MOSKA

77. FRONTISPIECE AND TITLE PAGE FOR VENUS AND
     TANNHÄUSER, 1895

Not so used. It shows the full title of this rococo novel.

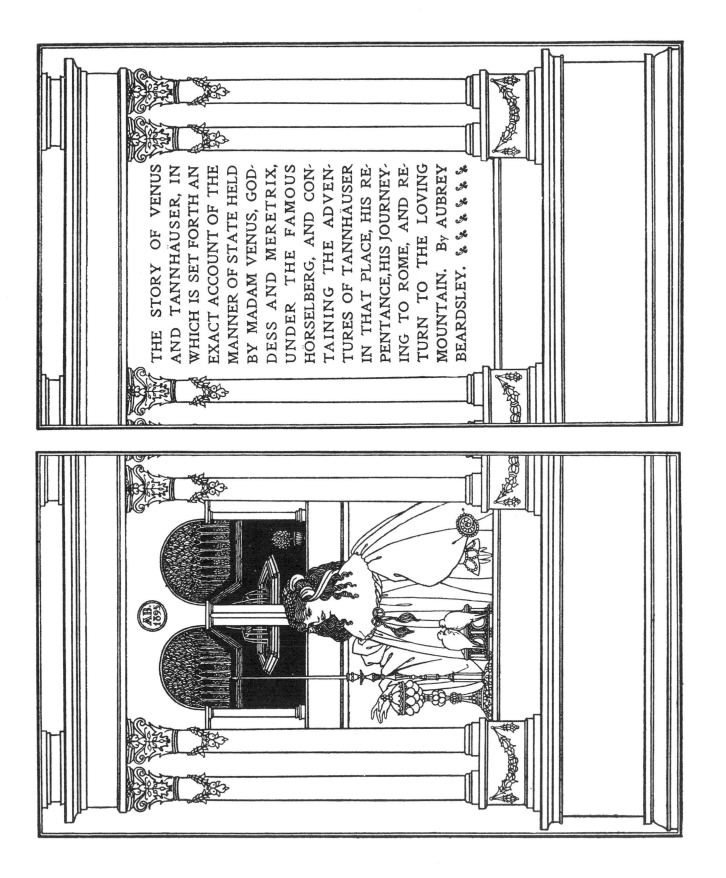

THE STORY OF VENUS AND TANNHÄUSER, IN WHICH IS SET FORTH AN EXACT ACCOUNT OF THE MANNER OF STATE HELD BY MADAM VENUS, GODDESS AND MERETRIX, UNDER THE FAMOUS HÖRSELBERG, AND CONTAINING THE ADVENTURES OF TANNHÄUSER IN THAT PLACE, HIS REPENTANCE, HIS JOURNEYING TO ROME, AND RETURN TO THE LOVING MOUNTAIN. By AUBREY BEARDSLEY.

78.   FRONTISPIECE FOR VENUS AND TANNHÄUSER, 1895

Not so used. Also called "Venus Between Terminal Gods."

VENUS.

79. THE RETURN OF TANNHÄUSER TO THE VENUS-BERG, 1895

A new version of an earlier drawing called "Tannhäuser," testifying to Beardsley's continuing interest in the legend which at that time he began to rewrite as a "romantic novel," *The Story of Venus and Tannhäuser*.

80. THE ABBÉ, 1895

From *The Savoy*, No. I. This drawing and the following five
are illustrations for *Under the Hill,* an expurgated version of
The Story of Venus and Tannhäuser which appeared in *The
Savoy*. Tannhäuser, meanwhile, had become the Abbé Aubrey,
then the Abbé Fanfreluche.

81. THE TOILET OF HELEN, 1895

From *The Savoy*, No. I. A repertoire of Beardsley's characters. Helen was the new name for Venus.

82. THE FRUIT BEARERS, 1895

From *The Savoy*, No. I.

83.   THE ASCENSION OF ST. ROSE OF LIMA, 1896

From *The Savoy*, No. II. *Under the Hill* became a receptacle for Beardsley's likes and dislikes, and a record of his current reading. Thus the Abbé is made to read the story of St. Rose of Lima, a religious transposition of Tannhäuser's flight from the earth.

84. THE THIRD TABLEAU OF DAS RHEINGOLD, 1896

From *The Savoy,* No. II. The Abbé also enjoys Wagner and sees *Das Rheingold* as a comedy, comparing Loge to Molière's Scapin.

85. THE FOURTH TABLEAU OF DAS RHEINGOLD, 1896

From *The Savoy*, No. VI.

86. THE COMEDY OF THE RHINEGOLD, 1896

Beardsley contemplated rewriting *Das Rheingold* as a comedy, as he had done *Tannhäuser,* and made this and the following drawings for it.

THE
COMEDY
OF
THE
RHINEGOLD

87. FLOSSHILDE, 1896

To illustrate *Das Rheingold*.

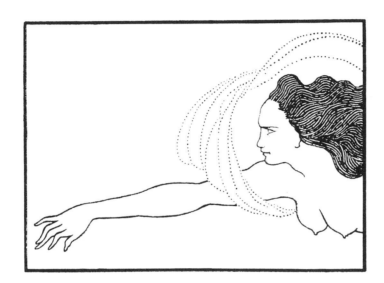

88. ERDA, 1896

To illustrate *Das Rheingold*.

89. THE DEATH OF PIERROT, 1896

As dawn broke, Pierrot fell into his last sleep. Then upon tip-toe, silently up the stairs, noiselessly into the room, came the comedians, Arlecchino, Pantaleone, Il Dottore, and Columbina, who with much love carried away upon their shoulders the white-frocked clown of Bergamo; whither, we know not.

90. THE COIFFING, 1896

From *The Savoy*, No. III. To illustrate Beardsley's suavely sinister poem "The Ballad of a Barber." The princess is shortly to be murdered, the barber to be hanged.

AUBREY BEARDSLEY.

91. TAILPIECE

For "The Ballad of a Barber," 1896.

92. COVER DESIGN, 1896

For *The Savoy,* No. VIII. The drawing was also printed in color and used as a poster by Smithers.

93. COVER DESIGN, 1896

For *The Savoy*, No. IV. The dramatic vertical division of the space was a much-favored technique of Beardsley's.

AUBREY BEARDSLEY.

94. COVER DESIGN, 1896

For *The Savoy,* No. V. Note Beardsley's use of a pseudonym as his signature.

GIULIO FLORIANI.

95. AVE ATQUE VALE, 1896

To illustrate Beardsley's translation of Cat

96. FRONTISPIECE, 1896

For *The Lysistrata of Aristophanes,* now first wholly translated into English (Smithers, 1896). These drawings, in Beardsley's own words "in a sense one of the best things [I] ever did" are, as Robert Ross wrote, "as frank, free and outspoken as the text."

The anonymous author of this translation praises (in a foreword) in Aristophanes the very elements which Beardsley himself no doubt appreciated and which are so much in evidence in his illustrations—"the ribald melancholy, this significant buffoonery, and the grotesque animality." Ross also excellently characterized the particular flavor, due to the combination of two powerful influences, not only of *Lysistrata* but of all of Beardsley's work at the time: "A real artist, Beardsley has not burdened himself with chronology or archaeology. Conceived somewhat in the spirit of the eighteenth century, the period of graceful indecency, there is, however, an Olympian air, a statuesque beauty, only comparable to the ancient vases. The illusion is enhanced by the absence of all background, and this gives an added touch of severity to the compositions."

LYSISTRATA.

97. THE TOILET OF LAMPITO, 1896

From *The Lysistrata of Aristophanes,* now first wholly translated into English (Smithers, 1896).

98. LYSISTRATA HARANGUING THE ATHENIAN WOMEN, 1896

From *The Lysistrata of Aristophanes,* now first wholly translated into English (Smithers, 1896).

99. LYSISTRATA DEFENDING THE ACROPOLIS, 1896

From *The Lysistrata. . . .*

100.   TWO ATHENIAN WOMEN IN DISTRESS, 1896

From *The Lysistrata. . . .*

101. CINESIAS SOLICITING MYRRHINA, 1896

From *The Lysistrata.* . . .

102. THE EXAMINATION OF THE HERALD, 1896

From *The Lysistrata.* . . .

103. THE LACEDEMONIAN AMBASSADORS, 1896

From *The Lysistrata.* . . .

104. A FOOTNOTE, 1896

From *The Savoy*, No. II. An amusing psychological self-por-
trait.

105. AUBREY BEARDSLEY'S BOOK PLATE, 1897

Never used by him but by H. A. Pollitt instead, probably one of the drawings in possession of the latter which Beardsley asked to be destroyed. Like "A Footnote" it is a psychological commentary on himself.

106. MRS. PINCHWIFE, 1896

For a projected edition of *The Country Wife* by Wycherley.

MRS PINCHWIFE

107. MESSALINA, 1895

Published by Smithers in *A Second Book of Fifty Drawings,*
first in 1899, then in a portfolio in 1906.

108. MESSALINA RETURNING FROM THE BATH, 1897

Later version, showing a change of style. Published first privately by Smithers in twenty copies, then in *A Second Book of Fifty Drawings*, 1899, then in a portfolio, 1906.

MESSALINA.

109. COUNT VALMONT, 1896

From *The Savoy*, No. VIII. Proposed title page to *Les Liaisons Dangereuses*.

LES LIAISONS DANGEREUSES.

BY
CHODERLOS
DE LACLOS

110. APOLLO PURSUING DAPHNE, 1896

A beautiful but unfinished drawing in perfect correspond-
ence with its border. The left foot was left in pencil and the
figure of Daphne was cut away. Made about the same time as
the *Lysistrata* set of July, 1896.

111. PENCIL SKETCH OF A CHILD, 1897

Showing, like "Apollo Pursuing Daphne," Beardsley's method of drawing firm lines directly on a blurred pencil sketch.

112. FRONTISPIECE FOR JUVENAL, SIXTH SATIRE, 1894

From *The Yellow Book*, Vol. IV. The various drawings made to illustrate Juvenal's satire on women met with a mixed reception on publication. The frontispiece was published in *The Yellow Book* but was not included in the portfolio containing drawings for the same work which Smithers published later (*An Issue of Five Drawings Illustrative of Juvenal and Lucian*, 1906). It was satirized in *Punch,* with a caricature of Beardsley pulling a cart.

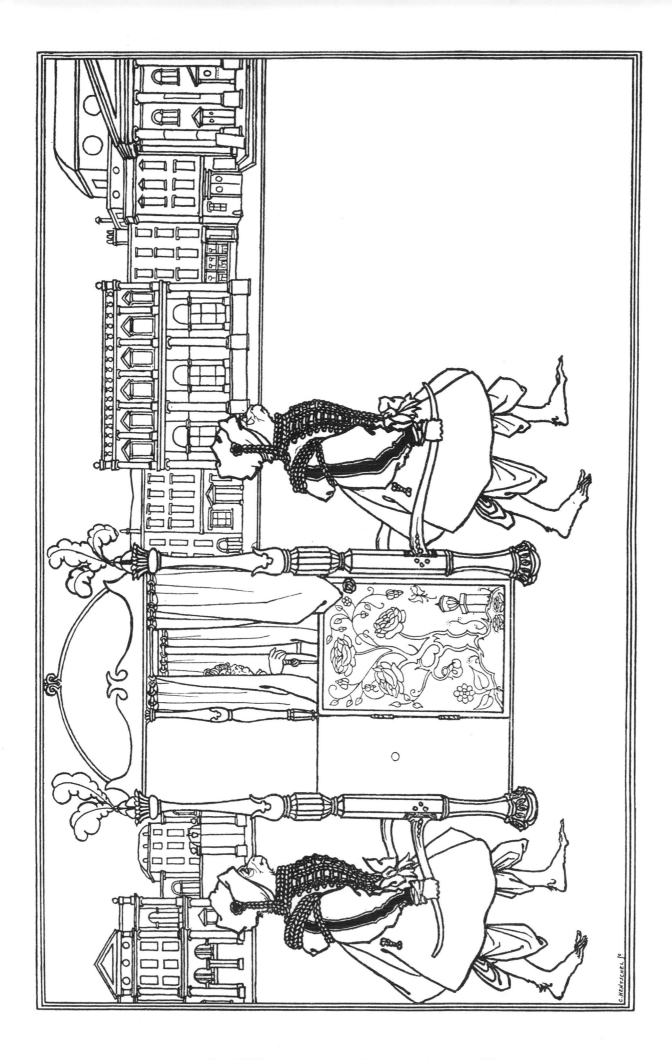

113. JUVENAL SCOURGING A WOMAN, 1897

First published privately by Smithers in 1897, then revised in the *Later Work of Aubrey Beardsley,* and finally issued in a portfolio with the following four drawings, by Smithers in 1906 (*An Issue of Five Drawings Illustrative of Juvenal and Lucian*). It shows, like the frontispiece, the influence on Beardsley of his early studies in architecture.

114. BATHYLLUS IN THE SWAN DANCE, 1897

Printed by Smithers, first privately in 1897, then in the portfolio of 1906.

BATHYLLVS

115. BATHYLLUS POSTURING, 1897

Printed by Smithers, first privately in 1897, then in the portfolio of 1906.

BATHYLLVS

116. D'ALBERT IN SEARCH OF HIS IDEALS, 1897

First published in a portfolio to illustrate Gautier's *Mademoiselle de Maupin* (Smithers, 1898), a novel much admired by Beardsley. It shows a change in the artist's favorite medium, pencil and wash instead of pen and ink.

117. THE LADY WITH THE ROSE, 1897

Included in the *Mademoiselle de Maupin Portfolio* but possibly not intended as an illustration.

118. FELIX MENDELSSOHN BARTHOLDY, 1896

One of a series of proposed caricatures of musicians. Beardsley also drew Chopin, Weber, Verdi, and Paganini.

119. BOOK PLATE, 1897

Olive Custance, a poet and contributor to *The Yellow Book*, and a personal friend of Beardsley, who later became Lady Alfred Douglas.

120. COVER DESIGN, 1898

For *Volpone* by Ben Jonson (Smithers, 1898). The artist's last cover design. Although dated Paris, 1898, it was finished in December, 1897, at Mentone.